Shantiniketan and Other Poems

Shantiniketan and Other Poems

Dr. Manorama Biswal Mohapatra

Translated by :

Dr. Jayanta Mohapatra
Prof. Prafulla Kumar Tripathy
Prof. Rohinikanta Mukharjee

BLACK EAGLE BOOKS
Dublin, USA | Bhubaneswar, India

Black Eagle Books
USA address:
7464 Wisdom Lane
Dublin, OH 43016

India address:
E/312, Trident Galaxy, Kalinga Nagar,
Bhubaneswar-751003, Odisha, India

E-mail: info@blackeaglebooks.org
Website: www.blackeaglebooks.org

First International Edition Published by
Black Eagle Books, 2024

SHANTINIKETAN AND OTHER POEMS
by **Dr. Manorama Biswal Mohapatra**
Translated by :
Dr. Jayanta Mohapatra
Prof. Prafulla Kumar Tripathy
Prof. Rohinikanta Mukharjee

Original Copyright © Dr. Manorama Biswal Mohapatra
Translation Copyright © Dr. Jayanta Mohapatra, Prof. Prafulla Kumar Tripathy, Prof. Rohinikanta Mukharjee

All rights reserved. No part of this publication may be reproduced, stored in a retrieval system, or transmitted, in any form or by any means, electronic, mechanical, photocopying, recording or otherwise without the prior permission of the publisher.

Cover & Interior Design: Ezy's Publication

ISBN- 978-1-64560-574-4 (Paperback)

Printed in the United States of America

*I dedicate this creation of mine
to my childhood memories....*

Preface

Places, relationships, nature, domestic experiences : these are the main sources of Manorama Biswal Mohapatra's poems. The print plight of Shanti Niketan Tagore's Dream-University saddens and infuriates the poet who admires its founding genious. Its dance has been stilled; devils and dragous have turned that sweet dream into a fierce nightmere. Its cry makes her listless, nostalgic about its glorious past that had initiated her into the art of poetry and music. This unrest soon grows into self-pity, she feels she is a woman in exile trying to climb up a broken ladder. The poet pays rich tribute to her mother who had first planted dreams in her : she never capsiges, never ceases to burn. There is a goddess in every mother, she says. Her decrepit village pains her as much as her house whose love and faith have given way to sadness and gloom. The poems, mostly, have an elegiac tone: yet there are moments too of hope and assurance of survival.

Prof. K. Satchidanandan
Eminent Poet & Professor of Malayalam Language
Ex-Secretary
Central Sahitya Academy

Pledge of Poet

I feel that a poet or any artist can live without God but he can not live without his faith, dream and the pain of living. I have been writing poems in Oriya since 1962. My poems often seem to compete with each other in a succession towards increasing maturity in form, content and style. I don't find a precise answer to the baffling queries. Why do I write? What and how do I write? This is probably the most exasperating effort for a creative and devoted artist to spell out an exact answer. I can, however, search, for, its answer, in fact, remains embedded in meaningfulness, if any, of my existence. I have experienced over these two decades or so, that poetry writing has been the only prop of my life on which the whole edifice of my existence stands. It gives me immense pleasure and a great release in particular though not in the form of romantic escapism. I have always been thrilled at the birth of a poem, which proceeds with an intense, emotional spasm converging on a blissful emotional relief. Often I don't search for words and in moments of trance they come to me, assume shapes, spring a kind of pulsated rhythm and beckon me.

I pride not at such esoteric origin of my poems though I simply marvel at them. Such candid impulses often play a game of hide and seek with me and ultimately usher me to an intimately private world where a selected flora and fauna exist. I get transported to an altogether different world of metaphysical heights where I perceive the underlying harmony prevailing all over the universe. This world seems to have opening into different corridors though not leading to the Rose Garden of Eliot. It indeed leads to a kind of mystic arena for communication with a Mightier Spirit and leave me mute and dazed.

Lack of security, overwhelming obsession with meaninglessness of life, circumstantial fetters and lack of distinct vision of reality have probably contrived areas of isolation, consequently loneliness has become inevitable.

Often such loneliness does have celebrating effect on me. It takes me to a seemingly Parnassian height but in most cases, it has a positive injurious effect on the psyche as it lends me a pessimistic look into life and its related activities-a search for something that I have lost though I don't know where have I lost it and I try to retrieve it though I don't know where have lost it and I try to retrieve it though I do not know when and how. This prevailing sense of losing and an aesthetic struggle for regaining dominate some of my works.

Various expressions in Nature have often made me mad. But strangely, instead of adoring the vastness I discover man as a tiny tot, a helpless babe swinging in the cradle. The cycle of Nature besides all its glory and jubilation has often become an arid landscape to house my feverish aching thoughts. So my poems on "Spring" have become a kind of swan-song instead of celebrating purple patches of vernal colour.

To me art is concealment. It is a complex spectacle of woman in colored texture. There is always a dimension of colour and sound in my poetry. Even when I paint loneliness, it virtually becomes a purple patch, full of sounds and voices. The agonies of life reflected in me are just like the reflections in a prism. What I observe, I emit in different wavelengths and different colors. I am angry but it is always subdued anger, presented in a fancy. My realism is a mixed one. My sickening thoughts often overpower my sensuous imagination. My poems search for a meaning. The sensed of loss suggested in my poems is revived with rich grandeur.

I have an obsession that I fail to translate all my feelings. I do not consciously imitate. My observation is not photographic, it is rather aesthetic.

To me, the poems are a piece of music set to forgotten tunes.

The spectacles that I envision are strikingly in a state of flux. They change swiftly in varying successions but they are linked up in stringed-beads of memory. Thus elements of nostalgia, reminiscences, faded whispers, less intelligible voices have probably become inevitable in all my writings.

We have now started moving towards the 21st Century. The course of contemporary life has been running so fast that the experiences of human beings are rapidly changing. This rapid change has brought in new perils to our experiences and newness to our viewpoints. The newness in our own selves, also extends to the society and the a world.

Modern life has been affected in two different ways. On the one hand, the miracles of modern science have made life very comfortable and enriching. On the other hand, the dangers of a nuclear holocaust have made life unsafe and helpless. In this age of high technology wars, survival has become the central aspect of human life. The age-old values of people are undergoing fundamental changes due to these factors.

In such a scenario, a poet is no longer a forecaster of the future. She/He is merely an ordinary human being whose life has no value and whose future is uncertain.

Today's poetry makes its environment its own place. Mankind's silent language gets buried in the pages of history and if today's' poet fails to bring out this silent language, then his creation would only give joy but won't be permanent.

Human beings are like useless appendages in this modern machine-dominated society. Notwithstanding the final victory of science, man is helpless. Today he is faced with a big dilemma and is eager to restore his old values, Once upon a time, the whole world, the entire mankind was the subject matter of his creativity. Today, every Tom, Dick and Harry is superior to him. His own problems have today become bigger than the problems of the world. Instead of his intelligence, he has to rely more upon his common sense. Instead of the world, his own immediate surroundings have become greater for him.

Instead of expressing his view on the experience of the entire mankind, he is today expressing views about his own experiences. This is the image of contemporary poetry.

Dr. Manorama Biswal Mohapatra

CONTENTS

My Very Dear Santiniketan	15
Morning in Santiniketan	16
Santiniketan is Hostage Today	17
Shantiniketan has not Changed	19
Shantiniketan Comes into My Dream	21
Brimming love	23
Along the Broken Ladder	25
In Banishment	26
Father's place	28
The Mother's Shadow	30
The Day We Shared Mother	31
The Time of Return	32
Shimla in Shivalik	33
Rohitaswa	38
At Time I Think	37
No Change	39
Face to Face with the Village	41
A Goddess within Every Mother	43
Call Me to Yourself	45
Maiden of Spring	46
House	47
Village from the Train Window	49
You Called Me a Poet	50
Thus One Day this Life	52
I Never Told You	54
Nothing has Changed	55
When will You Return from Exile?	56
The Day of Durga Puja	57
Puri (1)	59
Puri (2)	60
Puri (3)	61

Where are you Taking me Away?	63
Growing Up	65
A Few Days Ago	66
Broken Time	67
Don't Ask	68
February	69
Which Riskikesh? Which Mathura?	70
I'll Preserve All	71
Till I am Alive	72
In the Sculpture of Words	73
Waiting	74
When Rain Comes	75
Bhubaneswar	76
A Bomb will become a flower	77
Only a poet can dream	80
Your letters	82
Wishes	83
The silent clouds	85
Today at Puri	86
Baliapal doesn't know	87
After a long time	88
Why	90
With your aqueous fingers	91
She was n't feeling well	93
My village this time	95
Song of the solitary river	97
They will come back as clouds again	100
My whole life for him	103
When you are silent	104

My Very Dear Santiniketan

Today, perhaps, is the birthday
of the moon
the honey coloured moments of
my dreams and remembrances
this rain-drenched noon
of Santiniketan.
The rain has accompanied me
like my dearest friend
to Santiniketan for a visit.
In the blushing lips of
'Fagun badhu' among the groves
the sweet echoes of love.
This hour of blossoming petals
this wonderous noon,
my very dear Santiniketan
gets drenched in rain.
Whenever I compose on Santiniketan
I don't know why
I feel so sad, so helpless
as though it were no name,
but the soft bed of my consciousness.
where for some time
I became oblivious of the people and the
world.
I had sown the seeds of love
in this very soil.
Lo! today only I discover
it has turned into a towering tree.
on its huge wings
I can see myriad wonders.
Santineketan is a wonder indeed.
a dream laden landmass.

Morning in Santiniketan

Now it is dawn
the chirp and chatter of birds,
all through the night
a fatigued Santiniketan.
Long hours of frenzied debate
prolonged parleys,
platoons of police everywhere.
Santiniketan received me at Bolepur
yesterday.
and led me to this place
I know she doesn't feel alright now.
It is dawn now.
The train will reach Bolepur
in a short while.
I had been to you after a long lapse of time
Santiniketan.
You were dancing then
with anklets of rain on your feet.
So much of fragrance in this soil
such great intimacy of contact.
The birds beckon me,
I just don't know when
I shall meet you again.
I shall open before you
the box of unspoken tales
only then,
but today I run short of time
you too don't seem disposed to listen eithter.

Santiniketan is Hostage Today

Santiniketan is hostage today
in the devils' camp,
bathing in tears.

Brokers have already sold by auction
its aristocracy and honour.
Who is to save Santiniketan
from the clutches of dragons !
All, eager to save themselves.

In the midst of tremendous hustle
After a long time, I had been to Santiniketan
Saw in the bushy leaves of mango grove
a yellow-spring bird sitting in dismay
As it had forgotton to sing since long.

It didn't fly away, when it saw me
The devils had cut off its wings.

I remained speechless.
Cutting off wings of poets like me
in broad day light.
The devils enjoyed themselves
in self contentment.
That day tears rolled down
the eyes of sensitive trees.
Leaves of *kadam* tree didn't thrill,
flowers didn't blossom in *Bakul* tree.
Will the devils understand
the language of protest?

Today in the mid-noon crows, vultures
and foxes loitering around,
with humour and innuendo.
Resounding the whole world
in awful cry of death from very near.

Shantiniketan has not Changed

It is impossible to give away
My listlessness of long years,
as it is impossible
to throw away
from my mind
the beginning of
"Komala Gandhar Raga".
It is there within me
Playing its tune non-stop
For all these years.

In the world of poetry
at Shantiniketan
I had held the hand of silence
and I had drawn
Rabindra Sangeet
towards myself.

Those pictures appear
Very indistinct
these days.
All that was sketched
on the leaves and petals
of Shantiniketan.
How soon the batik waxed
Picture piece was lost,
How soon the chorus of
Rabindra Sangeet
rendered by colourful girls
was lost somewhere.

Shantiniketan has not changed
The practice of
Komal Gandhar Raga
Continues within me
Like those lost days,
After so many long years.

Shantiniketan Comes into My Dream

I have never kept a count
of what I got and what I gave.
I have dishevelled and brought
everything while coming back.

Morn and eve
brimming with memory
murmuring darkness
of the river
and at the end
enthralled love
mixed with tears.

Shantiniketan had
built within me
a bridge of
relationship mixed
with a deep sigh
while coming back.

The history of spring
was smeared on it.
I have never given anything.
of course I have
brought the moments of my success
of joy and grief
while coming back.

What more could it have given me?
Wherever I go today
I get to see its bright noon face
I get to hear the morning call
of birds
and I get to walk on a carpet
made of golden buds.
Shantiniketan comes into my dream
and calls me back
like a very close friend
like love
I have escaped swinging
till now
because I love
Shantiniketan.

Brimming love

and eagerness to embrace life
what else could it have given me.
Now at the dusk of life
I get to hear its call.
I could have gone that day,
but did you let me go
in happiness?

You stood on my way
and said, "Don't go.
Everything is here.
What more can Shantiniketan
give you ."

On another day
people afraid of light,
put thorn and sharp pebbles
on my path
and threatened
"Let's see how you can go."

Heaps of hindrances
I would have passed
to reach Shantiniketan,
I had to bear with every word
I had to enjoy
my happiness
Sitting under this tree.

I have heard tree throbbing

of its wavering leaves
and its expanding branches.

Time may forget me,
an Odia poet had set her foot
on the soil of this Shantiniketan.

Along the Broken Ladder

I think I will announce now
take off all ornaments of pride
from my body,
free all dreams from your fist
put all weapons inside your quiver,
what else is there
you can hold on till the end.

The green roads changing slowly
the tone imprisoned in the casket of
commitment
slowly gets breathless
the flowers don't blossom innocently,
as before.

The forest of thorns and cactus every where
somebody has hidden the ladder at your front
you have to climb alone
the broken ladder.

In Banishment

Whatever you wanted to hear
Now hear.
My absentmindedness, my restlessness
My pride in climbing the mountain
Unnecessarily,
Or about whom so ever you have taken
As a sectarian mark on your heart
So long –
Listen to all that
You don't count darkness as darkness
Neither you count light as light
I don't take it as a knot in my mind
As before.

After so many years
In this life of darkness and light
Mixing tear and blood together
I have come to understand that
You are just like a child
You feel happy whenever you like
And don't when you don't like
You have been shocked many a time
Because you can't beautify
Your talk.

Whether I am there or not
You go on asking for me everywhere—
Even to the walls
Just like a small child.
Enough of this life

These household affairs,
Like a miser you stored.
All your virtues, goodness and work,
Let them be whereever they are.
Let us be together
Let us take the banishment from life together.

Father's Place

The daughter arranged everything
Decorated the garden with
New flower pods,
Dusted off ill arranged bookshelves
With her own saree
Wrote the songs of life
On the flower marked carpets.
The Kanchan Flower that was long waiting
To be bloomed
Bloomed that day.

The smell of curry in the kitchen
Filled all corners of the house sweetly.
I prepared countless pickles for the daughter
Singed small fishes inside lettuce
Made balls of pigeon-pea paste, and fried
linhelbs,

She ate all happing
Very tasty she said
Just as in her childhood days.
Looked at her photos in the album
Alone at noon
Felt congingly for Rajnit, Narinder, Satyakam
Her school friends
The school days were not lost
She thought again and again.

All the days passed
How one does not know

The daughter was to return to her home
She came after many years.
Like a dazzle of dream in a spring twilight,
She went back..

The Mother's Shadow

We have never allowed the mother
To see the sun.
We have been rewarded many a time
Writing essays on the mother.

A patch of mother's shadow
Filled my childhood with fragrance
And in every particle of blood
In my artery
Planted lovingly the plant of dream.
What faith, longing, protection
In that shadow,
What innumerable consolation
In crossing the uneven road,

In my dissatisfaction, anxiety
In days when I am unhappy
In all that,
That shadow is like a strange
Fancy land
A limitless, lighted Milky way.
She is like a small floating boat in the
Measureless ocean
Like an oil-lamp in a thatched mud house
She never capsizes
Never stops burning.

The Day We Shared Mother

The day we decided to share Mother
there were neither stars
nor the moon in the sky.
At times
one could hear
simply the groaning of the sea.
That day,
along with our land and property.
we split up Mother
in front of everyone.

Half of Mother's care
went to Younger Brother.
The other half to Elder Brother.
In front of witnesses
we split up Mother.
Silent, like a deity
abandoned for immersion,
mother sat unmoving;
Waiting to be consigned to the sea
after the ritual was over.

The Time of Return

Who can hold someone back
when the time of return is near?
Neither can you, nor can I.

At times, I've been enthralled
inside this desire of mine
to embrace the glittering world
and at other times
have I sat downcast in the darkness.
To think this is my home
often makes me feel happy.

It gives me joy to feel
this is my home
when I pick the dried-up leaves
and the letters I've read already
on my desk.

I have sat alone in the balcony
in the soft, tender light,
at times eaten by loneliness,
and sometimes with my face
crumpled in the darkness.
Suddenly, today,
having known it's the time of return.,
you try to hold me back.
For when this time in near,
who can hold another back..
Can you, can I?

Shimla in Shivalik

The Name of the toy train
is Shivalik,
quite pretty,
flanked by slumbering hills,
In the valley between hills,
This toy train is very slow
Someone raised hand
to stop the train...
who was it,
the stream in the
whistle of a tiny bird,
or may be the long hand
of the Sun.
After a while it'll rain
the air is full of
this message.
After I came to Shimla,
rain also has followed me
this time,
Pari, on my lap, said
She would go all the way to
Bhubaneswar in this toy train.
When children like Pari
sit on my lap
Life becomes more joyful,
It seems, nothing more
is necessary in this life,
So beautiful are the days
of Pari's childhood,
Like pure sweet smelling flowers
In the small eyes of Pari

there is wonder and surprise.
On both the sides
there are wild flowers
and twittering birds.
Pari is just four years old.
September 18 is her birthday,
the same day
Lord Ganesh was born.
Sheets of papers
and colour pencils
in hand,
Pari will draw
lots of sketches
of hills, streams
and restive clouds
settled in Shimla.
Where do these clouds
reside, Papa
Where do they
sleep at night ?
Clouds, butterflies
birds and flowers
are all in the picture,
in the drawing book
of Pari.

Drops of dreams
have been smeared
on the trees.
Pari has come as a tourist
with her Grandma
to Shimla
in Shivalik.

Rohitaswa

A sudden cyclone
swept the village of Rohitaswa.

Rohitaswa, a student of class IV
was busy drawing a landscape
in the school.
The cyclone blew away
his drawing copy, school box,
water bottle, and of course
a small picture
of a picnic party beside a river bank
that he had drawn.

For surely someday
Rohitaswa could have been
a poet or a painter,
could have painted
River Subarnarekha
with word and colours.
That day the sudden cyclone
buried Rohitaswa
under the collapsing walls
of the school.

No, it hardly mattered
if he couldn't become
a poet or painter,
the cyclone whirled round
the school to bury Rohitaswa.
Apple of his parent's eyes

their only wealth,
Rohitaswa was
like a sacred shining
morning in a hamlet.

Now who shall read out
lines from the Bhagabat
and sanctify them
when their souls depart?
Who shall light
their funeral pyre
and console
their anguished bodies ?

Rohitaswa
only a small point of absence
in the cosmic void,
Rohitaswa
only a small thrill
lost in the super cyclone.

At Times I Think

At times I think of writing to mother,
but what would I write.
All the words have dried up long ago.
Sometimes I think of Mother,
she creeps crawling in the dark on all fours,
searching for so much..
Searching and weeping.

When Mothers cry in their grief,
I don't like it at all.
And still, such is their fate
that tears are only their very own.

God too hasn't understood
their fate till today.
At times I think of writing to Mother,
childhood was filled with wonder then,
just like autumn, when you would let me dream
of holding the falling moon in my hand.
I've still kept with care
that dream inside me.

Merely because I could not show my son
the dream of the moon,
he keeps on searching for gold mines.
Mother, the fruitful seed
you had secretly planted in me
in my enchanting childhood
had now grown huge,

shaped into a lovely tree.
Today,
my eyes are turned upward to the sky
I feel
at times I think of writing to Mother,
but what will I write in the letter?

No Change

No yet,
Neither the address
Nor the sketch of the house,
The festival of flowers in the garden
Continues.
Wherever I was
I remain there
No change yet.

Whenever I attempt to
Pluck flowers from heaven
Or to cross the river of blood
I have become speechless
Either in indifference or in sorrow.

Day in and day out
Deep in meditation
I have given a call to Ganga
The way to swargadwara is not far away,
I know
The souls of my ancestors
Have lighted this way,
This way becomes all colourful
As one passes.
One hears the indistinct twitter
All around,
In meditation, in wish fulfillment
Radiant is this way.

No change yet,
Neither the address

Nor the sketch of the house
I am here,
Only at time, a sad sunset shivers
On the top of my house.

Face to Face with the Village

After a long time
after many years
once again,
I have come to the village
and to the soil.
I was dreaming of the village
I was asking all around about it
again and again.

Now coming to the village
what do I see ?
Dry, like a stunted tree
and the dry, meaningless smile of children
and painful, helpless look of old men.

Who has stolen the noise
and the smiles
and the wealth?
I stood silently, in darkness, along
and listened to the piercing noise
of a night-bird
moving in the sky.
Who calls me in darkness?
Calls me by my childhood names?
She has a gold coloured saree
and she is no more.

I stand and listen
in darkness lost
away from the town

patting the memory of a
bright morning
in the village.

A Goddess within Every Mother

Soon as I step on
the threshold of our house
Mother's brocaded saree-end
wipes out the sweat drops of my gloom.

The flavour of her
shell lime and catechu-smeared betel
invades even the streets.

Mother is never in
the T.V. and V.C.R. Room
basking under the gentle sun
on the roof of our house
she makes badi
or exhausted she sits
in a corner of the kitchen.

Mother smells like a goddess,
Is she a goddess or a deity?

Sometimes she smiles and weeps
Absorbs pain
and turns into stone
like a goddess.
If goddesses are tortured
the lotus plants of faith are burnt
and ruined.

A goddess or a deity
stays hidden
in every mother.

Call Me to Yourself

I am grieving at unrest
and call me to yourself.

Grant me two eyes
and unbridle me
from my sightless inability.

Clutch me closer
and swear off
my vanity.

I am bereft of love,
call me to yourself
in my grief.

You are so engrossed
in the grandeur of your garden,
Why shall I go,
if you do not call ?

Maiden of Spring

The Spring Maiden is getting Keats, Shelley
and Tagore by heart.
The girl of the Spring
The sad and the lonely girl
memorising in the evening hours.

I'll go back to the harbour
Where I had anchored my beliefs
I had warned the girls before leaving
"Keep sitting here, girl,
Never think of the 21st century
Keep sitting within
the confines of this era
If you go beyond your mooring is lost."

The girl is very lonely
Like her mother
The girl is very proud
Like her mother.

The girl of the spring
Must be sitting
Alone with her sadness.

Today I'll return to my confines
To my home
Where I have wrapped
With care, my thoughts
in silk cloth.

House

On some days now
the house appears sad and gloomy.
Once love used to spill over
and turn into lotus of faith.

The fragrance of lotus
filled the whole house,
there are many islands in the house now,
without any light or air.

The skeletal trees
have taken away
the garden's charms,
now the house
feels so dead,
One who dreamt
of this house
hangs as an
oil portrait
on the wall.

Beneath the cloak of suspicion
love has turned into stone
like the prince of the folktales
faith has become helpless today.

No one needs it,
it keeps on sitting
or sleeping
just like old mother.

The lamp of faith
which she kept
burning in the niche of mud house
has been blown out
by someone's cruel hand.
At times
I feel like going
back to the house
just to lean against
the wind sweeping
through mint leaves.

I'll tell the islands
to preserve their
priceless love
within them
Love has become
Scarce today
On some days
the house
suffers great pain,
like a mother.

Village from the Train Window

What's there in the village
That calls you back?
Swarms of bees,
Miles and miles
Of golden mustard fields,
Shrill and lengthy calls of birds,
Tattooing
Days of childhood.

Standing in rows and
Saying prayers, "O, God
Lead me on the path
To Truth and Virtue"
What's there in the village
That calls you back?

The visage of the village
Looks so sad and morose
From the window of the train,
Someone calls me by name
At midnight.

I can make out the silhouette
Of the village road from here
The fragrance of lotus and water lily
Comes into the compartment
What's there in the village
That you insist on visiting it today?

You Called Me a Poet

You addressed me as 'Poet'
and enchanted me,
you called me a poet
and lightly touched
my tender inner emotions
my whole being
was fragrant with passion.

I kept on staring at the starry night
with my eyes wide open,
Writing poems
and living like a poet
are two dissimilar things,
at times
it is all blood and tear
at other times
it is sweet savoury honey.

I have been playing with words
for an eternity,
expecting an image of words
may be engraved in my consciousness.
I am an emotion-laden tree,
now full of leaves and flowers,
and moment from now full of blood and tear.

I dream at lot
because life is so pleasant,
my tears and indignation
become one at the same point.

How could you find out
my innocent feelings?
When you were sure nobody was listening
you whispered and called me a poet.

Thus One Day this Life

One day life
will end thus
drop by drop,
Only the boat will
stay put on the
river bank,
staring at the sky.

I know
I'll leave behind
all my favourite books
and albums
full of memories.
Life will trickle,
out thus drop by drop.

The oleander plant
will be laden with flowers,
a moonlit night will be
approaching and going way
from the river Salandi
of my childhood.

Yet, I am sure
I'll have to leave all these behind
and go one day.

I used to call the cloud
as a child, "Come cloud, come
Stop, rain stop".

Where is that cloud filled time
and where is my dear river?

I am nearing my end every minute
drop by drop.

Where is the cloud
and where is my dear river?

I Never Told You

I never told you
Why I didn't get sleep
The whole night yesterday.
In the thick dark
Only an unseen hairy hand
Called me out time and again.

The window was kept open
All through the night.
An owl hooted along.
Faint refrains of 'Raag Bhairavi'
Audible at once
Yet dissolved in air.

I did not press my eyelids
For once the whole night.
Some one like Mama
Clad in her golden 'Sari'
Stood at the dark root of a 'neem' tree.
The anklets of rain resounded all night.

The wall clock
warned in a hushed voice
Get up, get up
Life has neared its end.
I never told you
Why I didn't get sleep
Last night.

Nothing has Changed

I am present where I was
Nothing has changed;
Neither the address
Not the diagram of the house
Nor the festivities in the garden.

Whenever I had to ferry across
The river of blood through this path
I was struck dumb
In grief and resignation.
I have prepared myself
Night and day
To invoke the Ganga.
I know 'Swargadwara'
Is not very far from here.

This path has been lighted up
By the souls of my predecessors.
Whenever I walk
Through this path of fire
The whole world
Reveals itself in myriad colours.
Subdued chirp and chatter heard
All around.
This path turns into an avenue of fire
Through passion and meditation.

I am present here
Nothing has changed;
Neither the address
Nor th diagram of the house.
Only at times a painful sunset
Flutters on its top.

When will You Return from Exile?

When will you return from exile?
Once you come back
We shall together visit Puri.
I haven't seen a sunrise for long.
Together we shall see
The sunrise and the sunset.

Once you return
They would fish in the village pond.
Lord Shiva would be treated to
A grand holy bath
With one hundred and eight 'champak'
flowers.

I shall have occasion
To ask you in privacy
What did you do in your exile?
Were you charmed by the magic rainbow
Of a Maricha in disguise
Or of a Supanakha?

You know
Life in a village
Is like a honeycomb
Bulging with honey.
Tell me
When will you return
From exile?

The Day of Durga Puja

The house was silent as ever
Like the little girl.
On the walls drawn
Pictures of flowers,
Of the sun
And the river.
So many pictures she had drawn
With pieces of chalk.
No one knows
When they all grew moss.

Red and yellow lids of broken bottles,
Empty match boxes.
A piece of tiny pencil
Collected from school corridor,
She has left behind hidden
In her bookshelf.
Once she had stored all her dreams
Over there.
Like time, her parents have absconded.
Once her mother used to laugh and laugh
And again used to shed unending tears.
The house was thus silent as ever.

A day like that of Durga Puja
Left its fragrance somewhere
In her heart.

Now the girl desires to come back
Countless buds would be blossoming forth

The branches would break
Under the weight of flowers.
Whether one searches for her
Or not;
Calls her or not,
She would return to the dreams
Stored in her bookshelf.

Puri (1)

You too went to Puri
to forget your holidays;
fished out shells from the sea
and presented to your friend
Mita, alias Namita Das
on her birthday.

The sea is the pilgrimage of memories.
One who goes there for a holy bath
never comes back,
No use singing the age-old song
"The deer won't get caught
don't chase it in the hot sun."

If ever I go to Puri,
it will be to roll like a mridang
on your lion's gate,
the twenty-two steps leading to your seat
will be drenched
with the tears of my anguish.

Puri (2)

I too will not go toward Puri
to prickle my sorrow
to lie on the Baisi Pahacha
gazing at the Nila Chakra
and chant a mournful hymn.
The sea can produce diamond and gems
the tears of memories
and can wipe out many moments of my
memory
with its blue palms.
There is no point in drowning myself
in the sea of faith;
I will not return toward your Lion's Gate, O
Lord,
may be I will come upon a hippy girl there
once again.
You can go to sleep. O lord,
free from worries;
I will not beg any more for myself stupidly
I have no more complaints
I have already traced the distance
from the seaport to the coastline.

Puri (3)

What is this fragrance inside myself
In my soul
in my consciousness !

How I come into bud
bloom like a flower
on my own;
how I become fragrant on my own
like the sandal paste
like the burning earthen lamp.

Kalpabata, Shri Mandir, Swargadwar,
Snanabedi, Baisi Pahacha, everywhere
my consciousness spreads out like lotus petals
everywhere
pulsating and vibrant
like the bees at the dawn.
The three dimensional time
seems suspended from this tree
like the nests of tailor-birds
my fate, my future
dreams and memories
everything is hidden here.

After long days, Srikshetra pulls me in this manner,
the sea and the casurina groves
a patch of the tattooed sky.

I will perhaps come upon you

this evening.
How I come into bud,
bloom like a flower
in my inner self,
how I become sweet-scented on my own
like the sandal paste
like the burning earthen lamp
all alone
in the premises of the temple.

Where are you Taking me Away?

Where are you taking me away now?
Look at the countless perturbed eyes following me,
anxious and distracted.

Where are you taking me away now?
This is not the way I would leave;
the entire life was spent
bleeding
Where is blood left to save me
at this last moment?

Keep me for a little more time
It has been ages that I have seen
my white-hawk village of green earth.
Hold me up for a moment,
it has been a long time I have been
to the "Samadhi" of my father.
Don't you see my heart is heavy?
My kid brother has come
from our village to see me,
He has brought with him palua,
biri badi and cow-ghee
My grandma has sent.

Why do you take me away before time?
I have no wish to go at all,
How soon the time of departure arrives;
How can I go now

Leaving behind so much world
See, how the black cat has been fondly
cuddling up my legs
Since this morning.
How can I go now
at this unwanted hour?

Growing Up

I am turning out to be an adult
Gradually,
Despite all attention and care
My hair keeps greying.

In poetry-reading sessions
Or in this world of my own
I'll become evermore
lonesome
A kind of grown-up tone
Will cover all my
activities and speech.

If only a poet could
arrest time as she wished
There would not be
so much suffering in life.

A Few Days Ago

A few days ago
You were sitting in silence,
From the sound
Of the footfalls on the stairs
You could make out
Who came and went.

I was very busy that day,
I had promised,
But could not go,
It was just a few days ago.
Sensibility was the venue
At which we were introduced,
You also love the village folk
And the sorrowful girl
always drawing pictures.

Time will preserve
Your golden writings forever.
Your speech will be carved
On the life lived naturally.

Broken Time

There is a scare always
Over a lethal bomb.
The earthquake is talked about
Everywhere.

I had put together all my love
To make an idol.
Last night somebody
broke that.
When I try picking up
the pieces of the broken idol
I find my hands blood-soaked.

Don't Ask

You have snatched away
All my time.
Where is my own time
For writing a line
Or singing a couplet?
You lived for ever
Like an animal.
You never allowed me
to live as I wished.
You sought the reason
behind everything.
Today, when I am weeping
Please don't ask any questions.

February

Looking at the evening sky today
I remember the day
When the smell of wet soil
Mingled with the echo of green memory,
When the dozing earth
registered the pledge
of our paired lives.

The air full of countless melodies
Joys all around
And sweet sonority of
pure selfish love.

That was the only day
Marking the single truth
In my life full of failures.

Which Riskikesh? Which Mathura?

An amazing trance within you
A strange tonal hue dazzles,
You are a drop of water
Drawn into the sonic
immortality of time.

You were resplendent
In all the postures of surrender,
Ecstatic and complete.

Which Rishikesh or Mathura was it
That filled you with a trance
Beyond a moment in time,
Quivering and throbbing?

I'll Preserve All

What else is there
To preserve under sealed cover
Except those affectionate looks?

I have never asked you
In solitude, Angul,
Why did you call me
Into the vast and expansive
Wealth of your
Sal and teak forest?

All my ego, other-mindedness
Pretensions and artificiality
I have cast off,
I am a straight person
Very simple,
Gradually I spread into
All the sides of the horizon
Into the blue of the sky
And into
The hills and forests of Angul.

Till I am Alive

You made my inside picturesque
You draw inside me
With all its intricacies
A dream
That dazzles like a pearl.

I shall preserve
That soft and gentle dream
As long as I live.

In the Sculpture of Words

I have been waiting
all the time
For that one day
For that some day
When a cascade of
intricately sculpted words
Shall gush out of my pen
Like the babble of a child
Like the unhindered
flow of spring water
I shall witness
In the carvings of that sculpture
The advent of a beautiful dawn
Gradually descending on my psyche.

Waiting

Look here,
This morning
Like an innocent
tender child.

Far off there
That bird on the tree
Is speechless.

When it calls
All the doors within me
Open up by themselves.

All the time
I keep waiting
For that call.

When Rain Comes

I was a paper boat
Looking at the clouds,
Like those leaves in rain
I too had sprouted.

When the rain comes
Leaves sprout within me,
I become wholly green,
A narrow stream of tears
Flows within me.

Dreams and tears
Shatter me,
I am a tear-soaked Shravan,
I am buried
Within a mound of
Old memories.

Bhubaneswar

The rain clouds float away
Stroking the spire
Of your soaring temple.

Flowers of love do not bloom
In the cactus-minds
Of your sky-kissing flats.

The water of your Bindu Sagar
Swells with the tears
Of those dead centuries.

I feel, for me,
You are a Utopia
Hacking the trust-tree
And bringing together
The shreds again.

The empires of sorrow
Are quiet and desolate today,
Of no worth now.

Like a paper boat
I float across this city
Of Utopian wishes
In time squeezing like an octopus.

A Bomb Will Become A Flower

On the picturesque
Bosom of the sky
Expansive paddy fields,
Rows of fragrant mahua
And karanja trees
Green hills
Of all palm and coconut.

Inside all these
An innocent country face,
The face of Odisha
That under the yellow light
Of a wick lamp
Reads the Bhagwat every night.

That dyes the yarn
Making it
More colourful than dreams
That puts colour
Into wishes.

At times
Like the paddy fields at noon,
In its sad loneliness
Drinks down all the wants
And scarcity
If you come to Odisha
You will see
How the sky bows towards

The green paddy fields
In an embracing pose.

God is approachable for
Feelings here
He stands as a witness
When called by the devout.
Painted floors and walls
On festive days,
Villages girdled by
Shrubs and creepers
Everywhere the
Inner voice of Odisha
Everywhere the enchanted
Utterance of Odisha.

I love Odisha
She smells fragrant
Like a mother
I can discern from that smell
The circle of relations
I have preserved in my consciousness
The dazzling lines of poetry
Written by Phakir Mohan and Gangadhar
I love man
I want to extend my trusting hand
Towards man.

I want to build a world of faith
In this life.
Like the sacred hymns of the dawn.

If you attach a bomb
To the festoon of flowers
For shredding Odisha's soul
Into pieces
In an instant
It will turn into flowers
Here in Odisha.

Only a Poet can Dream

Who else but a poet
Can dream in hunger
And deprivation
O World?

The poet had imagined one day
India would turn into
A golden land
The mustard flowers
Would be field with honey
The fragrance of neem flowers
Would make
The blind bee
Forget its flight
I don't know
How and why it happened,
My heart breaks
In my utter inability.

What is this India
But a few lines
Drawn on a map?

The war at home
Has become more dangerous
Than the atmomic wars
Of America and Russia.

Blood flows on every road
Temples and mosques
Smell of gunpowder

Blood flows on every road
Religion is a mockery
Merciless murder of
Women and children
Continues in this land.

At such an hour
Who else but a poet
Can dream
That sounds hailing man
And life
Will be heard again
In temples and mosques?

Tell me, O World,
Who else can dream
More than the poet?

Your Letters

When your letters arrive every day
Sealed in memories
My blood is inflamed
And my world
Is filled with the sweet smell
Of Spring.

Today is not that day
Today is another day of grief
Despite the Spring all around
There are lost shadows
The visages of the trees and leaves
Look cheerless.

Today, a Sunday, is very cruel
Your letter will not
Come by express post
To scratch my memories,
You will no more be eager
To come back to me
On every holiday
Despite all the promises
Made in your letters.

Topics for talks are never exhausted
Letters come and go
I keep waiting like a solitary star
I know you'll never write to me again…
Do I have the good fortune
For a life after this life.

Wishes

As a child
Amazed at my own faith
I asked God,
"O God,
Take me on the path of
Virtue and Truth
I need nothing more
In this untrue and vain world."

Then I remembered those green days
Caring little for the scorching sun
Or the starry cold night
I traversed the chess-board of life
Defying all
I ran into untrodden
Desolate lanes,
Then I asked God
To grant me a dream
Of many possibilities and wishes.

Now is the evening of my life
And I wish to ask God,
"O God, this life and youth
This wealth is like
Water on the lotus-leaf,
Father, mother, brother and friends
Nobody is my own.

Make me, God, a couplet of a prayer song
That will make me forget
All my past failures
And will connect my memory
With all the other memories."

The Silent Clouds

The silent clouds
Descended to
Crystal white Tista that day,
By the time I left
They had begun
Gossiping atop Kanchenjungha
The Tiberan sky was
Moonless then,
Only pieces of cloud
Were loafing around,
The anxious say
Had descended all over the Tista
In wintry listlessness,
Everywhere was
A hint of rang bhairavi,
Bent with a load of fatigue
A bewildered being I am,
Many delicate feelings
Have been shattered
Without my knowing
In the harsh act of my living.

When I see a river or a hill
The delicate being within me
Wakes up at times.

Today at Pur

Your sweet tender love
Is strewn everywhere !
Soon after the rain,
It'll feel softer;
Drenched in rain
Jagannath will go to his aunt's house.

There his aunt's affection will
Drench him more
And he will look softer.
The sea unites everybody,
It unites all dreams and memories.

In what dream
Are you enchanted Natabara?
Your love-bird
Is no more hopping
In the branches
Of the wish-fulfilling banyan tree,
This time on my visiting Puri
I discovered
You too have flown far away.

Now, where do I search you out
At the Heaven's Gate?
Or in the sea?

Baliapal Doesn't Know

There are many things
Baliapal doesn't
Understand,
It is true that
The wind shall not
Caress the fragrance
Of ripe paddy,
Baliapal doesn't
Understand.

Why the blue sky
Turns blood-hued
At once,
Why mothers
Do not any more
Invoke the moon
To fall into
Small soft palms.
At night
When a leaf falls
It makes a thud
Of stones,
Conch-shells are
Blown,
Someone enters
Stealthily through
Hidden paths
At odd times
To plunder
The joys,
Baliapal doesn't
Understand all these.

After a Long Time

Today, after a long time
A red lily has bloomed
In a hyacinth-infested pond.

So very pleasing is this village
Faded walls of the huses
Mossy boundary walls
Draw me into their bosom
At school-going time.

I have returned
To my childhood
I have at once
Become a child
Khagendra, the school master
Mahendra sir
No one is their to day.

I feel happy when I come here
I get back all that
I have lost.

What is it that is there
In its moonlight?
In sheer human wants?
Unhealing wounds
Disappear at once when
Someone caresses me.

A red lily has bloomed
In the hyacinth-infested pond
Because I have
Came here after
A long time.

Why

Why since the beginning
Of time
Have you been burrowing
Your face in darkness?

I'll leave behind
Some golden memories
And also some dreams
For the time yet to come
Just for your asking.

I'll plant the tree
That smells as sweet
As our relationship
In your fragrant yard.

I'll ask the
Yellow love-bird
To build its nest
On the skylight of
Your bedroom.

Why have you been
Hiding in darkness?

Before a bomb drops
Today of tomorrow,
Soak your life
In loving.

With Your Aqueous Fingers

Touch me a little
With your aqueous fingers, Chilika,
Now, at these clouded moments
I am a piece of cloud
On the restless waves of water,
I am a ripple beyond the shore,
I am an engrossed bird
Hovering in the sky.

At a distance the twin hills
Soleri and Bhaleri
Appear as plantings
It's no very pleasant here,
This open sky
The shadows of the floating clouds
And the songs of the alien birds.

For a long time now
I'm not heard the song of the sky
So intensely,
I've never observed the Chilika
So closely.

I'll write down my name
On the waters of Chilika today
I'll write that
I came here
In search of a dream.

Touch me
Touch me a little more
With your aqueous fingers, Chilika,
Let me get close,
And closer to you.

She Wasn't Feeling Well

She was'nt feeling well,
For quits a few days
There was neither sleep
Nor ny dream in her eyes.

She had come
Hiding her dreams
In her pile of books.

With her mind engaged
Somewhere else
She was looking at the sky
A bevy of small birds
With chirping noise
Gave voice to
The morning and evening.

Layers of clouds
Like memories of her early days
Floated across the sky.

She wasn't feeling well,
Her baby-sister came to her mind
The sparrow learning to fly
From the skylight
Of her study room
Would have flown away by now.

The buds of yellow roses
Would have bloomed by now.

From the dark kitchen
Mama would be looking out
Into the pitch-dark night.
She would have turned
Herself into such a dark corner.

She wasn't feeling well,
There was neither sleep
Nor tears in her eyes.

Her father and mother
Were missing for a long time.
She felt a strange emptiness
The Puja vacation
Was approaching.

My Village This Time

When I visited
My village this time
Perhaps the birds were asleep
May be they had
No knowledge
Of my visit.

In the turmeric fields,
However,
The frenzied bees were
Flying to and fro.

The evening had just begun
When I arrived there
The chaurd smell
Of burnt lamp wicks.

A shy face peeped
From behind a door
And vanished inside
A gust of fresh flowery
Fragrance
Touched my memory.

She was from the
Neighbouring village
Now the Lakshmi of our family.

Treading her
Lotus-feet she has

Come to this house
Like a bride.

Her pink palms
And soft bright eyes have
Kept tied
This world of
Trust and faith.

For her
Every morning is
Suspicious,
Every moment is
Fragrant like a lotus,
Every sunset is
Enriched with
Sacred hymns.

This time
The house appeared
as heaven
I was getting lost
In unbroken silence
In wordless speech.
This time I felt
I had arrived
At a place of
No worry and care.

Song of the Solitary River

Now everything is placed and still,
A kind of solitude everywhere,
Time appears empty,
Only the wind whispers
Through the stalks of paddy plants
In the ancient corn fields.

Listless and neutral dialogues
Have been smeared
On the foggy paddy fields
This morning.

The tree you planted
Is now full of flowers,
You asked to cook
And went for a bath
To an unknown pond,
Never to come back again.

Did you fly away like a bird
To another and of this world?
You did not think
Of this world and the family
Flowing ghrough generations.

You left behind
The bright mornings
Woven with dreams and memories.

Amidst the troubles of
An ungrateful world
An artist was alive
Within you.
This world of words
Is silenced,
Evening-lamps are lighted,
Will you burrow your face
Between your knees
And like a poet
Stay put in untellable
Helplessness?

I ransack the darkness
In search of my childhood
And my past
Inside the womb of
Thrilling pain.

All that is odd and irregular
About me is because of you.
You allowed me my pride
And I appear
As a pampered child
In the pupils of your eyes.

Your mannerless sensitive
Daughter
Has learnt all the
Manners of an unconcerned life.
All the love of her childhood
Has been locked
Inside the safe of her mind.

You slipped away so silently,
Perhaps you remembered Mama,
Today I want to
Move round the fort of your love
Like a calf,
Nothing reflects my pampered self
As do your eyes.

They Will Come Back as Clouds Again

Where are
The dung polished courtyard
And the tulsi post
Of my dreams?
Where is my fragrant
Childhood?

Fragments of my soul
Along with my soft childhood
Fall from bomber planes
Over the village
Of multi-coloured
Flowers.

This is where once
My village used to be,
Like a rippling stream
Of golden hue
It used to move onward.

This is where
Inside this low-roofed house
My mother had entered
As a new bride.

She has not forgotten
The memories of
Her golden days
Of the days
When blood spilled.

My mother to
Smell of raw turmeric,
The raw dung and turmeric
Used to mingle as
One known smell.

The yard of our house
Resembled
The temple's main gate.

In the light of the
Evening lamp
My mother appeared
Bright as
The Goddess.

One may not believe it
But this is true,
My badma was
Saved from drowning
Here in this dark water,
She had tried to bring
An end to her life,
She was unable
To bear
The tortures of
Her husband's mistress.

There are no flowers and
Leaves now
Wherever one looks
Everything bursts into splinters.

The place has turned
Into a desert.
The eye of the villagers
Look bloodshot
The smell of gunpowder
And burnt coal
Has made nauseous
All these corpses.

These dead people
Will come down as clouds
To this barren earth
May be in their
Future birth.

I'll get to see them
In another planet,
Again the sun
Shall rise
Over this earth
A wonderful river
Will flow down
And enliven both
The banks.

My Whole Life for Him

If ever he comes under a silent sun
Dampening my eyelids
Or else in a heavy down pour
Of the month of Shravan
In the behag raga of the sarangi…

How would he know
I am not here any longer?
I burn like a wound
On some missile range by the sea.

Surely, he will come
The neem tree must have flowered,
Its fragrance drifting all around,
He'll grope for a lost childhood,
Will mope over it.
He couldn't have forgotten that
Childhood like a squirrel's back,
The village childhood
Full of neem and mustard flowers.

A quiet girl like a shadow
Red-hued like the manjistha bloom
A sullen sunset in her eyes
Will ask about me
And of other things
But how would she know
For whom
A whole life passed,
Waiting, waiting.

When you are Silent

I have been searching for a long time
If not for anything
Your affectionate eyes
That have caressed with the breeze
The trees, leaves and flowers of this house.

When I do not feel well
The very wish to have
A few whispered words
Under the krishnachura
For some time with you
Delights me like the
Overflowing waves of the foaming sea.

But when you are silent,
I forget the song of my life
And in my eyes everything
Turns smoky, dull and grey,
You know everything
And you know this fact too
That I am a misfit,
The familiar words of my speech
Seem quiet, caged in your ego.

If you are silent
I shall search for the flavor of youth in me,
In this calm, quiet room
And on the dark roof.

Black Eagle Books

www.blackeaglebooks.org
info@blackeaglebooks.org

Black Eagle Books, an independent publisher, was founded as a nonprofit organization in April, 2019. It is our mission to connect and engage the Indian diaspora and the world at large with the best of works of world literature published on a collaborative platform, with special emphasis on foregrounding Contemporary Classics and New Writing.

www.ingramcontent.com/pod-product-compliance
Lightning Source LLC
Chambersburg PA
CBHW060618080526
44585CB00013B/887